instagram @ivylis

midnight

tides

ivylis

for william"chicken"

i write these words to stay afloat
& i hope they can do the same for you

without the dark the moon would not shine

it is when the moon reaches the peak in the night sky
& you lay down to rest
that you feel the most at peace

you reflect on the reflections
from the tides of your past
as the moons
g
r
a
v
i
t
y
conducts the thoughts into rapidly flooding your
mind

the mist from the currents of your thoughts often

times fog the beauty of

your

life

the waves of life crash

& drag you under

sometimes only to giving you a few chances to catch

your breath

your life is a tsunami

& you are but a mere soul attempting to figure out

how to stop drowning

you are the

midnight tides

challenge the norm

break the chains

& set your self free

love eclipse

for a brief period of time
we became one
the moon felt the warmth of the sun
but only for a brief period of time

snap

in this life we try to be
so certain about certain things

so we refrain from taking risks that do not seem
absolutely promising
& often times we find that no matter how much

research we do
time we invest
or reassurance we receive
the outcome we portray fails to occur

although all the odds may have seemed as
though they were set in stone

 you have to remember that
even stone can be broken

journal entry

admire me
i
am art

porcelain

& you are just another victim
another shattered glass on the floor
just because i hurt you
does not mean i do not love you anymore
i can not help it
baby i am

b r o k e n

the cycle

i learned from the phases of the moon that

there are days where you will feel incomplete

but soon enough you will be whole again

vibes

watch what you speak into the universe

every word you say has so much more depth
than you can ever fathom
it carries a certain weight
it has an original vibration

when you speak something
whether it is negative or positive
it does not evaporate into the atmosphere
sound bounces off of objects
infinitely

the words you say
never go away
they drift
around creating the atmosphere
you live in each day

watch what you speak into the universe

clumsy love

do not put me on a pedestal
i will probably trip off
do not give me your heart
i will probably break it

sin

i know that it has to be a sin
to love someone so
then having to bear the pain
as you watch them go

bitter sweet

yes darling
the world is bitter
but you have to learn
to love the taste
of dark chocolate & black coffee
then life will seem so sweet

the muse of a poet

you no longer dwell
in the hallways of my thoughts
for once i put it on paper
the memories are lost

anesthetic

you carelessly said things
that meant everything to me
you meticulously cracked my heart
with each fib you told
but those cracks are now healing
without any feeling
i have become numb

moving on

so once again
our story begins
the same

you attempted to barge through the door to my heart
the one you would come & go out of so recklessly
but this time it was locked
& now only i hold the key

soul mate

& we are all
just soul searching
for another soul
to search
this earth with

journal entry

we were never official
now i am officially broken

unable

it does not register in my head
how you can say all you said
but still turn your back on the fact
that all you ever did was hurt me

so no we can not be friends

beautiful oxymoron

the beauty of love
is that
it is not so beautiful

equal

shame on you for not believing in me
&
shame on me for believing in you

roaming

my mind is torn apart
& lightly scattered in a million places

so give me a chance
to apologize in advance
for the trance
i tend to fall into

sleepless

late at night the ghosts
that hide during the light
creep up & find their way
into my mind

psa

ivory red headed goddess you do not need a tan to be beautiful
your snow like skin will smooth out any hardened soul

silk caramel queen you do not have to show your curves
to get a man
your personality will make any pure soul gravitate towards you

mocha chocolate sister let your natural hair flow
the coiled thread upon your head
will spring a statement to the world

latte arabian princess do not stray away
from the culture that raised you
you know how beautiful you are
you do not need reassurance from society

> *to all my sisters & brothers*
> *looking for inspiration*
> *i can promise you one thing*
>
> *you must embrace yourself*
> *& with that you will find your wealth*

alpha

you are an alpha

naturally weaker people will feel intimidated by you

some will gravitate towards you
others will stray away

do not be upset because of the ones that stray
you are not unaccepted
you are not rejected

this is a positive matter
for this naturally eliminates anyone who can not
vibe on your wavelength
but when you come across those rare gems who can

cherish them forever

journal entry

it is okay
to not be okay

ex marks the spot

now that i am gone you will search for me in everyone you are
with

i will be nowhere to be found

empty cups

i loved you as much as i love coffee

i am trying tea now

addiction

you are apart of me now
& i can not stand it
i can not stand the way i look at the smallest thing
& can not help but think about us
our nonexistent infinity

all i need is some help
but how is one suppose to receive help
if the only one that can fix you
was the creator of your very own hell

faster than flash

you always asked me
why i would take so many photos
in response i would laugh

now that it is over i guess you should know

i took so many pictures
because i know nothing ever lasts

wishy washy

part of you wishes you would have
never met them

while part of you longs to fall in love
with them once more

your indecisive nature is hurting no
one but yourself

twinkle

i smile at every person i am able to smile at
even if they do not smile back

a kind heart is contagious
& who knows
when that person who did not smile back at you lays down
to rest later that night
the only thing that may make them look forward to
another day
is the hope that another kind spirit will smile their way

deleted

although i unfriended you on everything
deleted all of our pictures
took every item out of my site that reminded me of us
i still can not manage to get rid of these memories

benefit of the doubt

i told myself
you were no longer allowed to hurt me
yet i still kept you in
hoping
you would live up to
the **lies you told**

then i realized

just that

they were lies

coping

you can not feel your face
i can not feel my heart
so i guess this is as even as it is going to get

illogical

how is it that you still cross my mind
when deep down i know you were the reason
why i lost mine

priceless

she is art
not the type you hang up in a gallery
& gaze at

she is the type of art that paints an ever
lasting image on your mind

she is the type of art that changes the
lens of your eyes

she is the type of art that changes your life

she is a master piece

self worth

if the sun is envious
of how deep the ocean can be
he would never be able to appreciate
the warmth he gave the world

32 below

the reason why we freeze food
is to keep them fresh

so what if we could freeze time
specifically those special moments

we would freeze them
so that those golden fragments of time
would stay just as they were endlessly

they would never decay away in the back of our
minds or become tainted by unfavorable
memories

they would remain the same shade of gold they
were the very instant they happened

if this were true
then maybe one day
i would unfreeze our memories
& come back to you

selfish

you once told me
everybody leaves *you*

but some how *you*
left *me* with no remorse

cautious

the devil comes in many different forms
it may not always be a storm
it can be something you have been praying for

worth

it is important to love yourself the way you are
for you are made from a bursting star
you are cut from the finest cloth
so when you feel the slightest
slice of doubt about your worth
fall into yourself & tell your brain

i love myself for who i am
for i know i was crafted
by the perfect hand
my flaws are not flaws
they are what makes me
me
i am beautiful
& you are a fool
if you do not see

visions

stop wasting energy on situations that only ever
give you a negative outcome redirect your focus
& begin your destiny

journal entry

i believe we as humans harp so much on attempting to
make life simple that ironically it begins to make our
stay here on earth complicated

fraudulent compassions

your inability to see the worth of a real thing
made you lose
your opportunity of spending
your life
with a real thing

loner

understand that

i do not mind being alone
i do not mind watching movies
alone
i do not mind shopping alone
i do not mind traveling alone
i do not mind reading alone
i do not mind drinking tea alone
but when i see
best friends laughing
two siblings relaxing
a child with their mother
a spouse with their lover

it makes me feel as though being
alone is not so great after all

fridaze

i love walking into book stores
& being surrounded by all the untold stories
waiting to be heard
the stories that take me
from the stressors of this world

kindred spirits

how do you know he is the one

simple
we operate on the same wavelength

one look & he knows what is on my mind
one smile & our love is defined

it must be because
we were from the same vibrational tribe

i am his kindred spirit
& he is mine

dial up

i feel so naive
i can not believe
i flattered you enough
to the point
where you became so confident

that you would see my phone call
& wait for it to quit ringing

shell

the best decision i have made thus far
was deciding to make decisions that were for me
choices that were souly for my soul
& not for society

so i can promise you
now that my shell is broken
i am never going back in

life time

in my boundlessly growing time line of life
you were present for an inch
how dare you think you know who i am

you do not know me
you knew who i was

journal entry

without disappointment
without heartbreak
without rejection
without loss
you would not be who you are today

u

you are not forever broken
just because you had to put yourself
back together in the past

you are not an opinion
you are not an option either
you should never let them define you
you define you
you are not going to fail

but you will be everything
you put your mind to

forecast

you will only disappoint yourself
comparing your struggles to someone elses

you can not compare
an earthquake to a hurricane

look up

you were so consumed in your work
you did not notice
my love
that bloomed
& illumined all night & day
it began to fade

you remained the same
consumed

here is some news for you

your work will fade the same way
 my love began to dwindle
that one winter day

now your work is gone
& so am i
you can get more work
you can not get another me

white

you are the type
of person
that leaves your mark
on whoever
you encounter

you do not know
how great
you truly are

for you stain their life
forever

eclipse

it is unfortunate that the sun
& the moon get to see one another so seldom

i am the moon
you are the sun
vibrant
glistening
you were the one

why did you have to go mr sun

i control the tides
now that you are gone
it is a tsunami

journal entry

if you are all over the place
nothing will fall into place

between the lines

o   ver
f   re

wings

i fell in unconditional love
you did not catch me
good thing i am a bird
& i know how to fly

chem 101

your love maturity level was revealed too late
    i had already bonded with our elements

shore

it is like she is the moon
& i am the tides
because no matter
how hard i try to flee
her gravity
will not let me leave
she always pulls me back

sierra leone

only a diamond covered pick
could break my diamond covered walls

sky

how do you expect yourself to fly
when you have all those things

weighing

you

down

nourishment

pick at my mind
i am a flower breezing in the wind
& my petals are full of knowledge

over it

you text me
i miss you
usually i would be ecstatic
however i am tired of your games
so i just simply
swiped
deleted
& moved on with my day

paper thin

do not crumble your feelings into a ball
then stuff them in the crevices of your heart
by doing that you clog the space
for the actual love you deserve
holding on to residual feelings
does you
 no good

take your feelings & express them
be unapologetic

so when that time comes
when you find the one
& you know they fit the part
they fill the crevasses of your heart

writers block

can
not
stop
thinking
about
you

journal entry

    i am emotionally unavailable

autobiography

my hair is a spiral of golden thread
perfectly placed on top of my head
my skin was dipped in the finest honey
& my eyes were drizzled with caramel
my soul was sprinkled with the shiniest glitter
my hands were cut from a satin cloth
my skin was kissed by the sun
but i was adopted by the moon

truth of love

i have always done things for me
what ever satisfied me

i did

what ever path i wanted

i pursued

i never thought
i would compromise
my happiness
for someone else

same old song

i fell for you
then you left me
how typical

i was so naive
& for that reason
i am stereotypical

pity party

you are trying to fill a hole
attempting to make yourself feel whole
not caring who you harm on the way

selfish

you have always been so selfish
that is why you chose to be with your self less

surrounded

the unfaithful people you surrounded
yourself with are doing nothing but damaging
your soul

realized

that you are no good for your own good
& you are definitely no good for mine

envy

i am comfortable in my darkness
just like the moon
but i can not lie
there are times
when i look at the sky
& secretly whisper
           i wish i was radiating brightness
                          like the stars

unruly

there he was the man that loved me unconditionally
& then there he was the man whose love for me
would come & go
 my heart yearns for the man that comes & goes
as i watch the man that loves me so
admire my every move
all i can imagine
is that being the man that comes & goes

if only the man that comes & goes
loved me like the man that loves me so

occupied

if you paid rent
for the space you occupied in my mind
i would be able to pay my actual rent

intoxication- the modern love story

i miss you

Read 3:50 AM

currency

time is the currency of life

you can not afford
to pay attention
to the negative essences that are in your atmosphere

you can only afford to invest in activities
that embrace yourself

you will find wealth is not a tangible item
it begins within yourself
but most importantly
you will learn that
you will never go bankrupt by being rich in spirit

lollipops

tell me something sweet baby
tell me something good
i am not trying to seem needy
but i want you more than i should

shatter

you would think
that once
you got your hands
on something priceless
you would try your best
not to break it

one bite at a time

> there will be moments that life knocks you down
> & your only resort is to start from the beginning
> this is such a beautiful thing for you have
> no where
> to go
> but up

learn to crawl

> you will have to become infant minded & look at life
> from a brand new perspective

learn to walk

> there is a reason why babies are fed milk
> for the simple fact that they are not ready to indulge
> actual food

learn to run

> so rebirth your mind
> drink the milk of life

then you can fly

take a seat

i would not say i hate you
to hate is to bear a burden on your soul
you do not even deserve my hate
so please
do not flatter yourself
by thinking that i hate you

???

icannotmakesenseofmythoughts
theyruntogether&donotaddup
whatismypurposeinlife
amidoingwhatiamsupposetobedoing
amiwhereineedtobe
icannotmakesenseofmythoughts
asdfghjkl

text back

why yes my love
i would love to love
the lovely feeling
of love once again

anastasia

i was dreaming for so long
longing for the day you would wake up & realize that i was
what was best for you

for a brief moment your indecisive nature began to cast a
spell on me

i unconsciously decided to wait for you

slowly
you reversed your own spell
 your lies began to wake me up from the deep trance i fell
into

i do not know which one is better

breaking free from your spell
or being heart broken as the result

max capacity

you do not deserve my forgiveness
but i forgive you
because you really do not deserve
to be on my mind any longer

tick tock

you take your time all the time

time is an essence we can not buy or get back
take your time to make sure its right
but *beware* there is a risk in taking your time

your lover will not wait forever
unmaintained love slips & sulks away
that may be the price you pay
when you take your time

blossom

you are comparing yourself to a
flower that has blossomed
many seasons before you

for you have just sprouted

you are so caught up on the
others success you are
remaining stagnant
you can not compare to which
you do not compete

steam

today i am drinking tea
i figured if i can physically refrain myself
from drinking coffee
i can mentally trick myself
into thinking of topics other than
y o u

money management

think of your tears as 100 dollar bills
it will finally register
they are not even worth a dime

luna

you are a moon child
shining in the dark
& you are able to move anyone
that steps into your light
like how you move the tide at night

the letter

there are some days where i just want to clock out
i want to take the time card of life
& stamp it one last time

i wonder who would wear all black
then show up to my funeral
just to post a picture on social media
saying how much i meant to them
& how they are going to miss me

there would be people who wished
they would have said the things
that they have been holding back
if so they would curse at their pride
& then proceed to feel sorry for themselves
but where were these people when i was alive
there were no where to be found
i was left alone to love myself

the response

i found her
& her letter underneath her favorite pillow
i wish i would have known the battles
she fought each day
we stopped talking a few months ago i missed her but
my pride would not let me reach out
i should have never held back my feelings
my thoughts or my actions
i regret the last words i said to her
i should have told her how beautiful she really was
how when she would smile my heart would skip a beat
but my pride brought me the worst defeat
now i am forever wondering what could have been

i loved her but she will never know that

gold lens

she is gypsy
moving so graceful
rarely ever sinning
she adores everything on earth
& attempts
to see the good in every situation

she loves a love that is going extinct

she looks straight into your soul
even if you were dark
she notices your gold

amusement park

it was the thrill
the give & take
the cold breeze followed by a burst of flames
the roller coaster of intimacy
reaching the peak
then plunging into another heartache

i was addicted
i was never in love

flow

constant unbearable tornadoes
would be the result if the leaves
& the wind were constantly anxious

instead they just go
naturally

they give us a beautiful sight
as they fly around the trees
leaving behind a soothing warm breeze

they flow
where they are destined to go
without questioning a thing

you should not be anxious
beautiful things happen naturally
so let life flow like a leaf in the wind

street lights

the dark alleys
of my mind
the ones
only the
moon can see
that is the place
where you dwell
that is where you
will
find me

begging for a hand

empty
            lying in bed
sinking
           into my own
infinity
     trying to remain afloat for i am
searching
        for my purpose in life

days pass
       closer to the day i will die
i do not want to
       feel as though i am dying
i want to feel
      as alive as possible but
i am sinking
       & i do not know how to stop
         i do not know
        no i do not know
         how to stop

natural

look around you
everything
beneath
beside
around
& above
you is hand crafted from the
hands of perfection

life is so beautiful

do not be the fool that takes the
natural gifts for granted

dead end

i cease my mind from
wandering into wondering
about whether or not

you miss me
you need me
you think of me
& overall
if you still love me

you did not allow me to be
the love of your life

i am now content
with being the loss of your life

metamorphosis

just because humans do not physically
go into a cocoon
does not mean
we do not go through
metamorphosis

question

is love a feeling or a choice

most would say that it was a feeling
& that is where most go wrong

if love is a feeling well feelings fade

just how you love the summer
or you hate the winter
depending on the day
the human mind is always changing
& priorities of life they are rearranging

i would have to say that it must be *a choice*
feelings come & go
you must chose each day to conquer the obstacles
one must commit to love

180 degrees

the clouds can only facade so much
the sun will eventually reign through
the darkness will only dwell somberly
for that moment in time

change your perspective
& that is how you will see
it is not as bad as it seems
you must turn 180 degrees

living paradox

mesmerizing like a fire
beautiful like snow
too hot to handle
too cold to hold

he is cursed

i wish i would have made her stay
i was foolish
stuck in the world
she was an enchanting rare breed
like an opal grain of sand
in her presence souls would mend
i was condemned
i missed my brief opportunity
my chance God sent
now its ever too late
now she is gone with the autumn wind

my apologies

pardon me
i am a hopeless romantic

bare with me
i still do not know who i am

get to know me
i am more than just a face

i have loved
i may have lost or forfeited
i am not quite sure

excuse me
i am indecisiveness

i can not pin point what makes me tick
i still have yet to figure out what i am here for
i miss every new opportunity
i accidentally close the opened doors

i do not even know how to end this poem

& i never finish anyth

zZzzZ

physically we wake up everyday
but a spiritual awakening
happens once in a life time

perks of my past

i have a lot of baggage
i have skeletons in my closet
i used to be ashamed of my past

but then understood
that carrying my baggage
has made me stronger

& i befriended my skeletons
seeing as they made me who i am today

back around

yes it is true
do good & good will come to you
but remember
it works the opposite way too

journal entry

wanting more for yourself
is the only way to get more for yourself

solitude

although i am surrounded by people
i feel just as alone
as when i am actually alone
that is why i chose to remain by myself
for the simple fact that joyous people
only remind me that i am not

empty

you are chasing these females
that are so shallow
the crew that you claim is so shallow
these clubs you are going to are so shallow
the cups of crown you drink
to numb your brain
so you do not
think about the pain
that is shallow

so i know when you are all alone
you feel empty like those bottles

little bear

what ever the weather
i would not mind
if we lay here forever
just you & i

falling in fall

love can not seem to fill
the gap of space between us
the atmosphere is thicker now
the leaves are turning brown
when it rains its floods
& this cold bitter night matches my mood
i did not want to become distant
because of the distance
but i could not stop it & you did not care
so here we are falling apart in the fall

pinky promise

i will draw your happiness
if you erase my sadness

hour glass

we recklessly flipped our hour glass
not realizing that time would pass
grain by grain
we were hypnotized
mesmerized with the energy of love
so our days were spent in a daze
 grain by grain
 we were careless
paying no mind to the deep hole
cupid was helping us dig
 grain by grain

i drifted deeper in love with the way you gave your vulnerable
love
grain by grain
the memories etched into our mentals
will never fade
they will just fall further into the files
of our thoughts each day
grain by grain
i was distraught when i saw our hourglass
 was reaching the last drops
but then i remembered

 love is timeless

no title

i never really
loved you
i loved the idea
of you
i loved the lies
you fed into my
head
i cared about
the person you
pretended to be
i was heart
broken on a
totally made up
situation that
never existed
because you
were never real
with me

i do

i wanted to be engaged to you
although the timing was not right

then it dawned on me
as if the fog from the morning
had suddenly evaporated

that i can get engaged in anything
i can be engaged in
traveling
good food
art
coffee
tea
self improvement
nature
books
absolutely anything

but not love
for love takes time
let love simmer
let love ride
feel the bumps
& live for the smooth
but do not rush love

noose

you may have to learn the hard
way when you hang onto
someones word
& not their actions

pop quiz

they will get on their knees
they will beg
they will plead
it is always the same routine
they will make it seem
as though they mean it this time
they will seem oh so sincere

you know how stay strong
this is the moment
you have been rehearsing for
the moment you knew was coming
it was inevitable
for they do this every other season
this is the book you have been studying
the toxicology of his love

science

she is the most introverted extrovert
i have ever met
she does not tell people about herself
or at least more than they need to know
& for that reason i do not know much about her
other than that she is a beautiful mystery
however
i do know one thing

we are opposing magnets
fighting our natural will to be with each other
& no matter how hard i fight
i can not escape the love i have for her

love & hate

i never know the suns intentions
sometimes he wants me to glow
& other times he burns me with his rays

smoke break

let me be your habit
your cigarettes
let me be the
thing you do on your afternoon break
let the thoughts of me consume your mind
i want you to ache for me

i soon realized that the down fall to being
someones habit
is that one day they will break you

origami

i am beautiful on the outside
i am intimidating to try
i am often afraid to show
the folds i consist of
i know for a fact
most would be taken aback
by my ins & outs

but
the key to unlock me is simple

persistence
take your time with me

i am mesmerizing
like the first snowflake of an anticipated
winter
as delicate as butterfly wings

so *be gentle*

i may just let you iron out my creases
& unfold all my reasons
 as to why i keep my secrets

journal entry

one day my success
will triumph all of my
failures

interracial

you are young lion aspiring to be the king of the jungle

i am a young princess waiting to be crowned queen of the
kingdom

for i love you despite what others say
we are different but the same in a way
& our separate cultures will soon become one

love has no boundaries

blink of an eye

i wanted to tell you
i love you
every silent moment we shared
just to be sure that you knew
it is too late now
our moment is gone

the journey

going up

> you shouted at me
> as i began to
> walk up the stairs
> towards the light

yes

i replied

i am the only one
who can fix this sorrow
for every other outlet
i tried has failed
there is no other way out
i must do this myself

home

like a ball that is thrown up in the air
like a boomerang thrown astray
like a homing pigeon flying away
like echoes in a dark hallway

i will always come back to you

birds fortune

today i am a bird

for they are not confined
to the nature of this man made world
they are not prisoners of politics
they are not slaves of money
they are not regulated by law

& when they want to leave a place
they simply just fly away without a trace

so i decided from this day forward
i will free myself from the chains
& every negative action or word

because today
i am simply a bird

journal entry

they all admire me
but none of them get to
know me

taken

i hope that the person that decides to take on the
challenge of loving me will not judge me based off
of what others say
i pray they will not care about the rumors that
spread
whether they are factual or false

but most importantly i want them to fall in love
with my soul
because physical beauty fades

braille

concentrate on me
slowly feel me
read me
memorize me

for i was made for you
& only you
to understand

satisfaction

do not love yourself too much
then you are conceited

do not hate yourself too much
now you are self conscious

do not go out & have fun too much
now you are a party animal & you can not settle down

do not stay in too much
now you are a hermit & you need to get out of your shell

at the end of the day
society is never going to be satisfied
so live for you

back wash

our cup
of love
i filled it
but when
you took
a sip
you spit
it out

recognize

you meditate

to fast forward the wait so you

medicate

yourself because
it numbs the pain you place a

barricade

on your emotions
to prevent another

heartache

but soon you will realize
that ignored pain
is just another

mistake

sprout

the flowers that you crushed
underneath your hostile steps
when you stormed out of my life
eventually grew back

they reminded me
that i will too

marks

the way your words hit my body
at a thousand miles an hour
those impacting words
seem to have left an ever lasting scar on my brain
so i am asking tonight

if you can talk to me without any words

if for once
my eyes would be able to physically see
the promises you so easily spoke into my ears

evidence

you avoid the void
not realizing
that avoiding the void
is a void within itself

tune in

when you are in tune with your soul you begin to feel certain
feelings that you have never felt before
you feel unfamiliar tingles
atypical thoughts
days become exceptional
& before you know it you have an unmatchable life

a life that is filled with remarkable moments
moments that words cannot describe
only feelings

trust me
if you have not already started
begin your journey
there is not better time than now

delinquent

how can you punish an adult
when as a child they never had a curfew

vaccine

no amount of antibiotics
can cure
this love
i have for you

cracks

we were laying in silence
my head pressed against your chest
you were embracing
every breath i would take
you were there for our relationship
through the moves
through the shakes
however that day
as i had my head against your chest
i could hear your heart slowly break
because you knew
the simple fact
that i no longer loved you

silence

the mind is an amazing thing
it has the power to create the most realistic vivid
descriptions of your fate

when i decided to follow my heart
i learned that my mouth was now my worst enemy
for it has the ability to jeopardize the very creation of my
dreams before they reach the point of existence

the visions of my future
my dreams
are contained in the most secretive way possible
in a discrete dimension
inside of the mind
with my skull acting as a soundproof barrier
that protects them from being heard by the world

it is the mouth that will destroy these dreams before they
even make it out into reality
my eyes are reminiscent of two way mirrors
 & my neck is that of a podium
holding my brain & holding my tongue in one

you realize that class is not always in session
everyone does not need to know
your every thought or every move
you must work in silence
for you & i both know
actions speak louder than words

warp

stop
stand still
& think
clear the clutter
you are on the brink of going over board
you do not want to fall into the waves
because once they take you
you can not escape
so please
stop
stand still
& think

gushy

he said

*loving you is like
biting into a cherry
sweet
juicy
& a little bit bitter*

shells

just as you feed your body
you must feed your soul
we are just souls with bodies
not bodies with souls

success

i am starving
for something
that food
cannot
fix

roses

in the mist of all the tears
i noticed the flowers on her casket
i could not help but see the irony in it all

we do not mind ending a flowers life
to decorate the death of another living creature

clouds

do not conform to the natural norm
just breeze by living life
do not second guess or try to impress
live in the moment & do what feels right

stay on your natural high
lightly floating through your life

time bomb

it is not that i do not want you
i just do not have time for another heart break

connections

> make it so that
> your soul
> is so full
> that your vibe
> is soulful

help

lately life has become a blur
i am trying to find out what is going on inside
but my vision is so foggy

i know it is pain that i am feeling
but
i do not know how to explain
the things going on in my mind
so i remain
silent

i wish that you knew
my silence is a cry for help
for i will never verbally ask for it

old soul

they want to go out
i want to stay in
they want to get high
& i am perfectly fine
with staying on the ground

calm waves

i lay down to rest
with nothing on my mind
i am content with the tides of my past
tonight
my waves are calm
they are not fast

the same feeling that can make you feel

so high

can also sulk you

so low

whether you want to believe it or not we are put

on this earth to love

it can be a person a place an activity anything

we as humans are meant to love

think about it

even the way we are physically created is an act

of compassion that is even more enjoyable when

you are in love

we think about

the love we deserve

the love we loss

or the love we are fighting for

we ache

we yearn

we toss

we turn

& it is *all in the name of love*

heartbroken & lost

i am here to say **embrace the pain**
something beautiful happens when you have
a broken heart
in your life your heart needs to be cracked
just so you can see inside yourself & begin to
figure out who you truly are

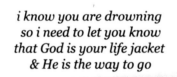

i know you are drowning
so i need to let you know
that God is your life jacket
& He is the way to go

CPSIA information can be obtained
at www.ICGtesting.com
Printed in the USA
LVOW11s0530060417
529690LV00001B/23/P